Gray Bat

Rod Theodorou

D1532650

Heinemann Library
Chicago, Illinois

Designed by Ron Kamen
Illustrations by Dewi Morris/Robert Sydenham
Originated by Ambassador Litho Ltd.
Printed in China

10 09 08
10 9 8 7

Library of Congress Cataloging-in-Publication Data
Theodorou, Rod.
    Gray Bat / Rod Theodorou.
        p. cm. -- (Animals in danger)
    Includes bibliographical references and index (p.).
    ISBN 1-57572-270-4 (lib. bdg.)   ISBN 1-58810-445-1 (pbk. bdg.)
    ISBN 978-1-57572-270-2 (lib. bdg.)   ISBN 978-1-58810-445-8 (pbk.bdg.)
     1. Gray bat--Juvenile literature. 2. Endangered species--Juvenile literature. [1. Gray
bat. 2. Bats. 3. Endangered species.] I. Title.

QL737.C595 T44 2001
599.4--dc21   00--063262

Acknowledgments
The author and publishers are grateful to the following for permission to reproduce copyright
material: Ardea/Martin W. Grosnick, p. 4; Bat Conservation International, p. 21; Bat Conservation
International/Brian Keeley and Annika Nicklaus, p. 23; Bat Conservation International/Merlin D.
Tuttle, pp. 6, 5, 9, 11, 12, 13, 14, 15, 26, 27; BBC/Lynn M. Stone, p. 4; Bruce Coleman, p. 7; Eye
Ubiquitous/Adina Tovy Amsel, p. 25, Eye Ubiquitous/Tim Hawkins, p. 24; M. Gumbert & J.
Macgregor, pp. 8, 17, 22; NHPA, pp. 16, 18, 19, 20; Doug Perrine/Seapics, p. 4.

Cover photograph reproduced with permission of Bat Conservation International.

Every effort has been made to contact copyright holders of any material reproduced in this book.
Any omissions will be rectified in subsequent printings if notice is given to the publisher.

Some words are shown in bold, **like this.** You can
find out what they mean by looking in the glossary.

Contents

Animals in Danger

cheetah

leatherback sea turtle

whooping crane

All over the world, more than 25,000 animal **species** are in danger. Some are in danger because their homes are being destroyed. Many are in danger because people hunt them.

This book is about gray bats and why they are **endangered**. Unless people protect them, gray bats will become **extinct**. We will only be able to find out about them from books like this.

What Are Gray Bats?

Gray bats are **mammals**. Bats are the only mammal that can fly. Their wings are like your hands. They are made from thin skin that grows between the bat's long fingers.

There are over 900 different kinds of bats, and many of them are in danger of becoming **extinct**. Half of all the kinds of bats that live in America are **endangered**.

What Do Gray Bats Look Like?

Grey bats are medium-sized bats. They have tiny eyes and cannot see very well. They find their way in the dark using **echolocation**.

Gray bats have toe claws that act like hooks. This helps them to hang upside down from the ceilings of caves, where they are safe from **predators**.

Where Do Gray Bats Live?

Where gray
bats live

Gray bats live in the United States of America. In the summer they live in caves that are close to rivers or **reservoirs.** They have to live near water, because that is where they feed.

In the winter, gray bats leave their summer caves and **migrate**. They find small, deep caves where they **hibernate** all winter in safety.

What Do Gray Bats Eat?

Grey bats are **insectivores**. They eat the insects that gather over water at **dusk** and night. They hunt mosquitoes, moths, and especially mayflies.

Gray bats find their **prey** using **echolocation**. The bat catches the insect in a flap of its wing and then snaps it up in its mouth.

Gray Bat Babies

When gray bat **females** are two years old they are ready to have babies. Each female has a single blind baby.

When the females have their babies they fly off and stay in a different cave with other mother bats. These are called **nursery** caves. The **male** bats all stay in the **bachelor** cave.

Caring for the Babies

These are bent-wing bats. Like them, gray bat mothers feed their babies milk. The babies cling to their mothers. They cannot fly, so they need to be close to their mothers to stay warm.

After about four weeks the babies make their first flight. They stay close to their mothers for another month, until they are good at flying and hunting their **prey.**

Unusual Gray Bat Facts

Gray bats help us because they eat a huge amount of flying insects. A single bat can eat 600 mosquitoes in one hour! Gray bat **colonies** eat billions of flying insects every week.

At **dusk,** gray bats leave their caves and fly through the trees to the water to feed. The path they take is called their **travel corridor.** If a travel corridor is cut down the bat colony may die.

How Many Gray Bats Are There?

Once the gray bat was one of the most common of all American **mammals.** At **dusk,** people used to see hundreds of bats flying off to feed.

In 1970, there were over two million gray bats in America. Six years later, in 1976, there were only just over one million bats left.

Why Is the Gray Bat in Danger?

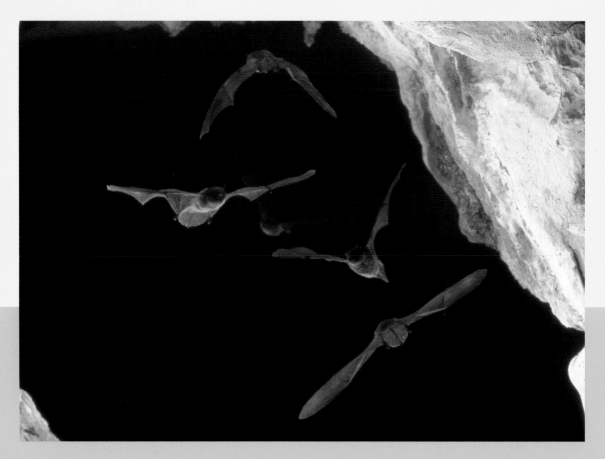

Gray bats have to find special caves to live in, especially in the summer. They have to be near water and where it is not too cold. Almost all the gray bats in America live in just nine caves.

When gray bats are disturbed by people they sometimes drop their babies on the cave floor and fly away. The babies die from the cold. The entire **colony** may never return, and may die.

In the 1970s **caving** became very popular and even more bat **colonies** were disturbed. **Travel corridors** were also cut down, causing many bats to die.

Farmers use special chemicals to kill insect pests. If bats eat any of these poisoned insects they may be poisoned, too.

How Is the Gray Bat Being Helped?

The U.S. Fish and Wildlife Service owns some of the most important gray bat caves. Other **conservation** groups are buying more bat caves.

These caves are protected by fences, gates, and signs. The good news is that the gray bats living in the caves are healthy and are having babies.

Gray Bat Fact File

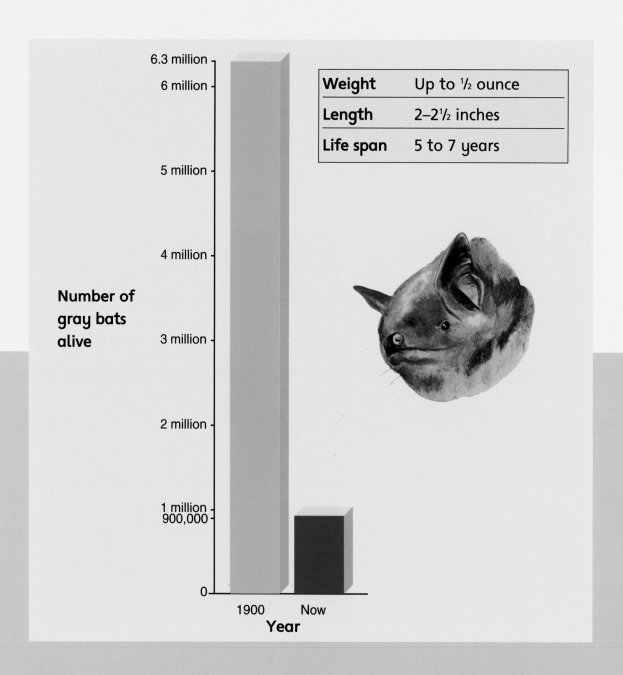

Weight	Up to ½ ounce
Length	2–2½ inches
Life span	5 to 7 years

Number of gray bats alive

6.3 million
6 million
5 million
4 million
3 million
2 million
1 million
900,000
0

1900   Now

Year

World Danger Table

	Number when animal was listed as endangered	Number that may be alive today
Gray bat	2.25 million	about 1 million
Flying fox	The flying fox is not endangered.	150,000
Indiana bat	about 800.000	about 350,000
Mariana fruit bat	less than 50	425–500
Ozark big-eared bat	200	1,800

There are thousands of other bats in the world that are in danger of becoming **extinct**. This table shows some of these animals.

How Can You Help the Gray Bat?

If you and your friends raise money for the gray bat, you can send it to these organizations. They take the money and use it to pay conservation workers and to buy food and tools to help save the bats.

Bat Conservation International
P.O. Box 162603
Austin, TX 78716

Defenders of Wildlife
1101 Fourteenth St., N.W. #1400
Washington, DC 20005

Organization for Bat Conservation
1553 Haslett Rd.
Haslett, MI 48840

World Wildlife Fund
1250 Twenty-fourth St.
P.O. Box 97180
Washington, DC 20037

More Books to Read

Gibbons, Gail. *Bats.* New York: Holiday House, Inc., 2000.

Sway Marlene. *Bats: Mammals that Fly!* Danbury, Conn.: Franklin Watts, 1999.

Theodorou, Rod, and Carole Telford. *Bat and Bird.* Chicago: Heinemann Library, 1998.

Glossary

bachelor   male animal that lives alone

caving   sport of exploring caves

colony   large group of animals living together

conservation   looking after things, especially if they are in danger

dusk   time of day just before it gets dark

echolocation   finding things by sending out a sound and listening for the noise that bounces back (the echo)

endangered   group of animals that is dying out, so there are few left

extinct   group of animals that has died out and can never live again

female   girl or woman

hibernate   to sleep through winter

insectivore   animal that eats insects

male   boy or man

mammal   animal with hair, like a human or a dog, that drinks its mother's milk as a baby

migrate   to move from one place to another

nursery   place where young animals are looked after

predator   animal that hunts and kills other animals

prey   animals that are hunted and killed by other animals

reservoir   place built to hold a lot of water

species   group of animals that are very similar

travel corridor   path through trees between a bat cave and the water where the bats feed

Index